NEWFOUNDLAND: A TASTE OF HOME

Cookbook and Travel Guide
Featuring Selected Bed and Breakfasts, Hospitality Homes,
Country Inns and Their Special Recipes

Rosalind Crocker

Blueberry Press
Mount Pearl, Newfoundland, Canada

Enjoy the book!
Rosalind Crocker

NEWFOUNDLAND: *A Taste of Home*

Cookbook and Travel Guide Featuring Selected Bed and Breakfasts, Hospitality Homes, Country Inns and Their Special Recipes

by Rosalind Crocker

Publisher and
Distributor

Blueberry Press
P. O. Box 612
Mount Pearl, NF A1N 2X1

ISBN 0-9697247-0-5

Cover
Graphics
Logos, etc.

Patrick MacKey
Rosalind Crocker
Reprinted with permission

Printed in Canada

Order Form - see page 112 (last page)

DEDICATION

*To the travellers who are inspired by adventure
and apply it to their cooking*

THANKS

*Patrick MacKey, Linda Hickey, Joyce Matthews, Anu Varsava
Wayne Tilley, Shirley Crocker, Edgar Sparkes, Ann Bell
Mark Vivian - Dept of Tourism, Computer Science - MUN
Gary Ryan - Y Enterprise Centre, Janie Davis, Alice Hollohan
Barbara Gamble, Ursula Mjolsness, Yvonne Parsons
all Participants and My Family*

SPECIAL THANKS

Patty Tibbs

and

*Nancy Creighton and Staff
Women's Enterprise Bureau, St. John's, Newfoundland
without whom this project would not have been possible*

Though we travel the world over
To find the beautiful,
We must carry it with us
Or we find it not.

- Ralph Waldo Emerson -

CONTENTS

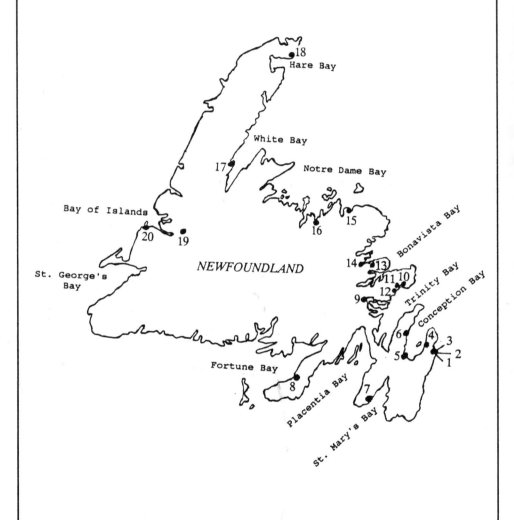

Hare Bay

White Bay

Notre Dame Bay

Bay of Islands

17

16 15

NEWFOUNDLAND

St. George's
Bay

20 19

Bonavista Bay

14 13

11 10
12

9

Trinity Bay

Conception Bay

6

4 3
5 2
1

Fortune Bay

8

Placentia Bay

7

St. Mary's Bay

KEY TO MAP

INTRODUCTION

Knock, knock, knock! Opening her front door and smiling at the stranger, the lady cordially replies, "Welcome to our home."

Newfoundland is our home and we welcome you to learn about our heritage and experience our culture. An easy way is to spend time at our guest homes, meet the people, taste our food, visit our historical sites and participate in our traditional activities. Every community and home is unique, and their brand of hospitality is, indeed, very different. That's the beauty of it.

Overviews and sketches of Bed and Breakfasts, Hospitality Homes and Country Inns accompany their special recipes to give you a little insight into what you can look forward to as a guest. There are suggestions for things to do and places to see in and around their communities, as well as, phone numbers, addresses, and a map for easy reference. Do visit the ones that sound appealing to you.

The book is also comprised of a collection of recipes that have been passed down and around, to and from friends, relatives and their friends. The origins of many of these recipes are unknown and similarities are unintentional. Numerous recipes are "from scratch", while others are creative and have been modified by the cook to reflect the availability of ingredients in the cupboards at the time of cooking.

Food is a symbol of hospitality and is an easy way to impress your guests. You are encouraged to use your own creativity in adapting these recipes, such as dessert at breakfast and fish for brunch. Breakfast is making a comeback and people are bypassing convenience foods for "real" home cooking.

I hope that the spills and smears on the pages in the book mean that it is used over and over again, as a cookbook and as a travel guide. Be adventurous!

BREAKFAST

Hospitality guests love a healthy breakfast. Many of these recipes are light, containing bran, yogurt and fruit, while others are a little heavier, depending on your taste. They are delicious and easy to make!

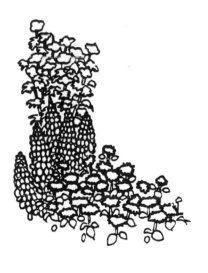

BROILED MAPLE GRAPEFRUIT

½ grapefruit for each guest
Maple syrup
A strawberry or cherry to garnish

Use grapefruit knife to cut fruit into sections. Spread a tablespoon of maple syrup on exposed side. Place under broiler for 5 to 6 minutes or until edges start to brown. Garnish with strawberry and serve hot. *Try other syrups such as cherry, strawberry or raspberry.*

WHOLE WHEAT CINNAMON PECAN TOAST

3 tbsp unsalted butter, softened
3 tbsp finely chopped pecans
2 tbsp brown sugar
2 tsp ground cinnamon
8 slices whole wheat or white bread

With a fork, mash together butter, pecans, sugar and cinnamon to make smooth paste. Under broiler, toast slices of bread on one side. Turn them over and toast very lightly on other sides. Remove from broiler, carefully spread topping on lightly toasted sides and continue broiling until topping is hot and bubbly. Let topping cool and settle slightly before eating. Serves 4

BREAKFAST BERRY CRÈME

1 cup whipping cream
1 tbsp plain yogurt

In a jar with a tight lid, stir together cream and yogurt. Close the lid, wrap jar in a kitchen towel, and leave it at room temperature overnight. Before serving, chill about 1 hour. Stir well before serving. Makes about 1¼ cup

STRAWBERRY RHUBARB MUFFINS

1 cup rolled oats
1 cup bran
1 cup strawberry yogurt
½ cup vegetable oil
½ cup brown sugar
1 egg
1 cup flour
1 tsp salt
½ tsp baking soda
1 tsp baking powder
1 tsp ground cinnamon
¾ cup chopped rhubarb
¼ cup white sugar
½ cup sliced strawberries

Soak oats and bran in yogurt. Add oil, brown sugar and egg. Beat well. Stir in dry ingredients. Sugar coat rhubarb. Toss rhubarb and strawberries in wet mixture and mix lightly. Bake at 400°F for 20 to 25 minutes.

BREAKFAST FRUIT CURRY

2 sliced pears
1 sliced banana
½ honeydew melon, 1-inch pieces
½ cantaloupe, 1-inch pieces
2 oranges in sections
10 dates, halved
1 cup grapefruit juice
1 tsp mild curry powder

Combine ingredients and refrigerate 2 hours. Serves 4

BONNE ESPÉRANCE HOUSE

20 Gower Street
St. John's, NF A1C 1N1
(709) 726-3835
No. 1 on map, page 6

Bonne Espérance, a charming Victorian home built in the 1800's by fishing Captain Whitely, is the pride of its owner, Ann Bell. Her home is filled with antique furnishings and heritage artifacts traditional of the Newfoundland craftsman. Picture yourself stretched out in front of your bedroom fireplace or curled up with your favourite book in the sitting room.

Exercise buffs, do a "walk about" on the trails and waterways nearby. Celebrate St. John's Regatta, held early August since 1826. A must to see - Signal Hill historic park, a spectacular view of the harbour city and Atlantic coastline. Experience the past - watch the Military Tattoo re-enact the colonial military exercises dating back to the Napoleonic Wars. Photograph puffins or tour the lighthouse at Cape Spear, the most easterly point of North America.

Next, visit our historical sites, cathedrals, museums, art galleries and shop downtown. Taste stuffed salmon at a fine dining restaurant and treat yourself to an evening of entertainment on George Street.

History and hospitality - a very special place to stay!

PARTRIDGEBERRY MUFFINS

2 cups flour
½ tsp salt
2 tsp baking powder
½ cup sugar
½ cup butter
1 cup milk
1 egg
1 cup partridgeberries

Mix dry ingredients and cut in the butter. Then add milk and egg. Stir to mix only. Toss in berries and mix lightly. Spoon mixture into muffin pans. Bake at 375°F for 18 to 20 minutes. Makes 18

The secret to these delicious muffins is to use lots of berries. Instead of partridgeberries, substitute carrot, pineapple or other muffin fruit. To vary the recipe, Ann often uses 1½ cups flour and ½ cup bran to replace the 2 cups of flour. If using blueberries or raspberries, you may want to use less sugar because of their natural sweetness.

APPLESAUCE BRAN MUFFINS

1 cup bran (or ½ bran and ½ oats)
1 cup buttermilk or sour milk
1¼ cup smooth, unsweetened applesauce
¼ cup molasses
¼ cup oil
1 egg
1 tsp vanilla
1½ cups flour
½ cup brown sugar
1 tsp salt
1 tsp baking soda

Mix bran, buttermilk, applesauce, molasses, oil, egg and vanilla together and let stand 5 minutes. In another bowl, combine dry ingredients. Add bran mixture, stir to moisten. Bake at 375°F for 20 minutes. Makes 12

EGG and BACON PATTIES

4 eggs
1 chopped small onion
5 slices crisp bacon, finely chopped
½ cup old cheddar cheese
1 cup dried breadcrumbs
½ tsp dried parsley
1 tsp oil

In bowl, beat eggs. Stir in onion, bacon, cheese, bread crumbs and parsley. Heat oil in a large fry pan. Add large spoonfuls of mixture, flatten slightly, cook 3 minutes, turning once. Drain. Makes 10

TOASTED WALNUT OATMEAL CEREAL

4 cups water
½ tsp salt
1 cup course oatmeal
¾ cup shelled walnut pieces
4 tbsp unsalted butter, cut in pieces
¼ cup brown sugar
½ cup heavy cream
½ cup fresh blueberries

In medium saucepan, bring water and salt to boil. Stirring continuously, pour in oatmeal. Reduce heat and stir until oatmeal thickens, about 5 minutes. Simmer and cook 30 minutes, stirring occasionally. Preheat oven to 400°F and toast nuts on baking sheet in oven for 7 to 10 minutes, just until they begin to darken their natural color. When oatmeal is thick, stir in walnuts and butter. When butter melts, pour into heated serving bowls. Sprinkle with brown sugar and top with cream and berries. Serves 4

FRUIT and NUTS CEREAL

1 cup rolled oats
½ cup chopped fruit (dried apricots, apples, or prunes)
2 tbsp chopped toasted nuts (almonds, walnuts, or pecans)
2 tbsp wheat germ
1 tbsp light brown sugar
1 cup skim milk or 2% milk
½ cup plain yogurt (optional)
Cinnamon to taste

In a large bowl, combine the first five ingredients. Serve in bowls with milk. Let stand 10 minutes for soft cereal. Top with yogurt and sprinkle with cinnamon. Serves 4
Store dry ingredients in tight covered jar in a cool place.

A GOWER STREET HOUSE

180 Gower Street
St. John's, NF A1C 1P9
(709) 754-0047
No. 2 on map, page 6

The Newfoundland Historic Trust designated "A Gower Street House" as a point of interest within the St. John's heritage properties. Hints of old English charm are visible everywhere... beautiful stone cathedrals, colorful hanging flowers, narrow hilly streets, and stately Victorian lamp posts stand in front of the adjoining clapboard houses.

The city offers speciality shops, craft shops, antique stores, art galleries, and museums. Enjoy traditional music in a nearby restaurant or pub, then take a leisurely stroll along the picturesque waterfront.

Great places to see... Cabot Tower on Signal Hill and the lighthouse at Cape Spear. There's boat tours - a city harbour cruise and whale watching. During the tourist season, a professional travel consultant is on staff.

Breakfast is served at 8 o'clock. Special rates available. Private off-street parking.

Leonard, David and Kimberly look forward to your visit.

NEWFOUNDLAND FRITTATA

2 cups fried vegetables and meat filling
Chopped green pepper
Finely chopped green onions
Sliced mushrooms
2 tbsp olive oil
1 or 2 crushed garlic cloves
6 eggs
¼ cup milk
Salt, cayenne pepper, black pepper to taste

Heat oil and garlic in heavy skillet over medium heat. Add filling, green pepper, green onions and mushrooms. Heat until warm. In separate bowl, beat eggs and milk with a fork for about 30 seconds, then stir into heated mixture. Add seasonings. Stir again after two minutes. It should be ready to serve in a few more minutes. Serve hot with toasted home made bread.

FILLING SUGGESTIONS (leftovers): Cooked potatoes, brewis (Newfoundland hard bread cakes that have been soaked and cooked), ham, bacon. Toss in green pepper, green onion, mushrooms or just about any combination you like. For a variation, we sometimes use lightly cooked salted codfish instead of the meats, but keep in mind that its flavour will permeate the dish.

Leonard mentioned that his recipe originated at a skiing party when an enterprising Corner Brook girl filled her skillet with food leftovers and scrambled in the eggs. Similar to an Italian dish, but has our local flavour. Experiment and enjoy!

CAPTAIN'S BREAKFAST

1/3 cup chopped onion
¼ cup chopped green pepper
¼ cup margarine
6 oz chopped ham
2 medium potatoes, cooked, cubed
½ tsp salt
6 beaten eggs
2 tbsp water
Dash of pepper

Fry onion and green pepper in margarine. Add ham, potatoes and ¼ teaspoon salt. Cook over medium heat about 10 minutes, stirring occasionally. In bowl, combine eggs, water, remaining salt and dash of pepper. Pour over ham mixture in fry pan. Set on low heat, occasionally turn until eggs are set. Serves 6

SWEET GINGER CANTALOUPE

2 ripe cantaloupe, halved, seeded
  and scooped with melon-baller
1½ tbsp honey
1 tsp finely grated fresh ginger
1 tsp fresh lemon juice

Put cantaloupe balls in a large mixing bowl. Add honey, ginger, lemon and toss gently to coat fruit. Cover with plastic wrap and chill for 1 hour. Stir well before serving in small bowls. Serves 6 to 8

PECAN STUFFED FRENCH TOAST

4 oz cream cheese
1 tsp vanilla
3 tbsp pecans, coarsely chopped
2 tbsp sugar
1 loaf day-old French bread, unsliced
3 eggs
¼ cup water or milk
Vegetable oil
Cinnamon and/or nutmeg

Blend cheese, vanilla, nuts and half the sugar. Slice bread in 1½-inch slices and cut a pocket in each centre. Spread a tablespoon of cheese mixture in each pocket. Mix eggs, water and remainder of sugar. Dip bread and soak in mixture a few minutes. Fry in oil until sides are golden, sprinkle with spices. Serves 4 *Top with maple syrup or fruit sauces.*

BAKED EGG and TOMATO CUP

2 large firm tomatoes
4 tbsp crisp crumbled bacon or chopped ham
2 eggs
Salt and pepper to taste
Bread crumbs

Cut a slice from stem end of each tomato and hollow out the pulp. Line bottom of tomato cups with bacon or ham. Crack open an egg and pour into tomato cup. Repeat for second egg. Season and top with crumbs. Place in dish and bake at 300°F for 30 minutes, or until eggs are set. Serves 2

BEACHY COVE BED AND BREAKFAST

P. O. Box 159
Portugal Cove, NF
A0A 3K0
(709) 895-2920
No. 4 on map, page 6

A short distance from St. John's and snugly tucked away from the hustle and bustle of the city, Beachy Cove Bed and Breakfast extends a warm welcome to everyone. Comfortable bedrooms, spacious living room and large balcony overlooking this little cove in Conception Bay, make it easy for you to relax.

Stand on the balcony, take in deep, deep breaths of fresh ocean air. Study nature firsthand... sea gulls gliding... osprey diving... whales blowing... and more.

Hike Princess Mountain Path to Greyman's Beard for a panoramic view of the ocean. Strike up a conversation with the friendly fisherman or try beachcombing! In the distance Bell Island awaits - only a stone's throw away, and you can accomplish a return day trip using the ferry boat service.

When the day is done, watch the fiery sun set across the bay and in the morning wake up to a hearty breakfast.

A promise of peace, quiet, good food and enjoyable conversation. A true bed and breakfast!

EGGS BEN-E-DOUG

English muffins, split and toasted
Fried ham, generous slices
   (size smaller than muffin)
Poached egg, one for each Ben-E-Doug

2 tbsp margarine
2 tbsp flour
Pinch of salt (optional)
Dash pepper
1 cup milk
¼ to ½ cup very old grated cheddar cheese
1 tbsp parmesan cheese

CHEESE SAUCE: Melt margarine in sauce pan over low heat. Blend in flour, salt and pepper until smooth. Add milk. Stir until texture is consistent, then add cheeses. Stir until texture is smooth again. Makes 1 cup

On your breakfast plate, layer muffin with fried ham and poached egg. Pour sauce over top. Serve with hash browns and sliced tomato.

Doug usually gets second requests from his guests for these. Absolutely delicious! Shhhh, cheese is the secret ingredient.

FRESH RASPBERRY OMELETTE

½ tsp salt
1/3 cup milk
8 beaten eggs
2 tbsp butter
5 tbsp wheat germ
1 cup raspberries

Add salt and milk to eggs and mix. Heat butter in pan until foamy. Pour eggs into pan and stir gently one minute. Sprinkle in wheat germ and berries. Cover and cook over low heat until set. Fold omelette over, cut in half and serve. Top with whipped cream. *Use blueberries and strawberries as well.*

SNOWY EGGS

3 egg whites
3 tsp vegetable oil
2 tbsp low-fat cottage cheese
1 tsp fresh green onions, minced
¼ teaspoon arrowroot powder

Combine all ingredients, beating lightly. Add 1 teaspoon vegetable oil to nonstick pan at medium heat. Add egg mixture. Cook without stirring until edges set, then stir from outer edges to centre. *Do not stir too much or use the heat too high because the eggs will get watery. Top with fresh fruit.*

WHOLE WHEAT BRAN PANCAKES

1 cup bran
1 cup whole wheat or bleached white flour
½ tsp salt (or to taste)
2 tsp baking powder
1 tbsp vegetable oil
2 eggs
1½ cup milk
Berries or chopped apples, optional

Mix the first four dry ingredients. Add the remaining ingredients and stir until well mixed. Pour on a hot fry pan or griddle and cook until bubbles show through. Flip pancakes and cook until other side is golden brown. Makes 9 to 10

CINNAMON APPLE BUTTER

4 lb peeled, cored, chopped cooking apples
¼ cup butter
1 cup sugar
3½ tsp cinnamon
5 whole cloves
1¼ cups water

Cook all ingredients in large saucepan over low heat until apples are very soft. Remove cloves. Beat mixture until creamy. Bring to a boil. Pour into warm sterilized jars and seal immediately.

THE STATION HOUSE

P. O. Box 117
Clarenville, NF
A0E 1J0
(709) 466-2036/2008
No. 9 on map, page 6

As you munch on Una Durant's cookies at The Station House, browse through their collection of railway, logging and boat building artifacts. The jacuzzi and sauna downstairs will relax your aching muscles after hiking or an exhilarating day on the nearby ski slopes. Then, pull up the foot stool and sip a glass of wine in front of the fireplace. Warm weather speaks for itself. BBQ on the large patio deck overlooking the bay or relax with a favourite cool beverage.

Newfoundland's wild flower, the pitcher plant, represents Brian's outdoor adventure company that offers bicycle, canoe, and sea kayak tours. Now that's different.

For a change of pace... perhaps you would like to play a few rounds on the nearby golf course, take a day trip to the national park or tour the Bonavista Peninsula.

Get ready for a "scuff" during their winter carnival or summer festival. You may even learn to play the spoons. Guaranteed good "time".

A bed and breakfast for all seasons!

BAKEAPPLE PANCAKES

1½ cups flour
1 to 2 tbsp sugar
3 tsp baking powder
½ tsp salt
1 beaten egg
1¾ cups milk
2 tbsp vegetable oil
1 cup bakeapples

In large bowl mix dry ingredients, then add egg, milk and oil. Add berries last, then mix only to combine ingredients. Heat griddle or fry pan to 380°F. Grease lightly. Use ¼ cup batter for each pancake. If batter thickens, add more milk. Cook pancakes until surface is covered with bubbles and edges lose their gloss. Turn over once and cook until golden brown on both sides. Serve hot, with butter and your favourite syrup. Makes about 12 (4-inch) pancakes

The Durants also make these using fresh or frozen blueberries or partridgeberries. Always a winner any time of the year!

TOUTONS

White bread dough
Oil from fatback pork, or margarine

Cut small pieces of bread dough and flatten about ½-inch thick. Drop in frying pan using oil from fried fatback pork. Brown on both sides and serve with butter, molasses, lassy coady, applesauce or jam.

LASSY COADY

1½ to 2 cups molasses
3 tbsp butter

Put in saucepan and bring to a boil. Serve over dumplings or toutons.

PEACH MARMALADE

6 oranges, peel from 3
24 peaches, peeled and cubed
9 cups sugar
1 cup chopped cherries

Chop the peel from 3 oranges in food processor. In saucepan add chopped orange peel, juice of 6 oranges, peaches, and sugar. Slowly bring to a boiling point. Then boil rapidly for 30 minutes. Add cherries and boil 5 minutes. Cool and preserve in jars.

MOLASSES BUNS

3½ cups flour
2 tsp ginger
½ cup butter
1 tsp baking soda
½ cup warm water
1 cup molasses

Stir flour and ginger. Rub in butter. Add soda dissolved in warm water and molasses. Roll out and shape in buns. Grease pan, bake at 375°F, 15 to 20 minutes.

PORRIDGE BREAD

1 cup rolled oats
2 cups boiling water
1 tsp salt
1 tbsp shortening
2 tbsp brown sugar
½ cup molasses
1 package yeast
½ cup warm water
4 to 5 cups flour

Mix rolled oats, boiling water, salt, shortening, and brown sugar. Add molasses and let cool to "warm". Add yeast which has been dissolved in warm water. Add some of the flour and beat well. Add flour to make a firm dough. Knead well. Let rise until double in bulk. Shape in loaves and put into greased pans. Let rise again until doubled. Bake at 375°F for 50 to 60 minutes.

EDGEWATER INN BED AND BREAKFAST

14 Forest Drive
Steady Brook, NF
A2H 2N2
(709) 634-7026/3474
No. 19 on map, page 6

What does the fringe of Marble Mountain and the shoreline of the Humber River have in common? The Edgewater Inn Bed and Breakfast, of course! Wintertime, gazing through the livingroom window, you can see the colorful skiers as they dip and turn down the slopes. Summertime open the patio door, take ten steps and cast your fishing line for salmon and trout. The upstairs balcony is private for aprés ski gatherings or just relaxing in the sun with friends. Any season, morning time... listen to the symphony in the trees and keep your eye trained across the river for visiting moose.

Today, let's... Windsurf at Pasadena. Jet boat on the Humber. Picnic in the park. Splash in the natural swimming hole. Find the beaver dam along the nature trail. Enjoy a horse-drawn carriage or horseback ride. Spend the day at Gros Morne National Park. Shop in the city... You decide! There is also merriment and dance at the Hangashore, Strawberry and Steady Brook festivals in July. What about the "man in the mountain"? What is he guarding?

Arrive as a guest... leave as a friend!

EDGEWATER SCONES

2 cups flour
4 tsp baking powder
2 tsp sugar
½ tsp salt
4 tbsp butter
2 eggs
1/3 cup milk or cream

Mix and sift dry ingredients. Cut in butter with pastry blender. Add beaten eggs (with small amount of egg white reserved), add milk or cream. Remove to floured board. Pat or roll to ¾-inch thickness. Cut into rounds, squares or triangles. Brush the tops with reserved egg white and sprinkle with sugar. Bake in hot oven at 425°F for 15 minutes.

RHUBARB CHERRY JAM

5 cups chopped rhubarb
3 cups sugar
1 package cherry jelly

Toss rhubarb in sugar and let stand overnight. Next day, heat to a boil. Cook 10 minutes at this heat level. Take off stove and stir in jelly. Put in sterile jars and wax seal. Makes 6

Scones are mouth-watering. Try them with Mildred's home made jelly. M-m-m-m good!

PAULINE'S TEA BISCUITS

2 cups flour
2 tsp baking powder
½ tsp salt
½ tsp cream of tartar
2 tsp sugar
½ cup shortening
1/3 cup milk

Sift first five ingredients together in a bowl. Cut in shortening until mixture is crumbly. Add milk to bind mixture. Roll mixture out to ¾-inch thickness. Cut in shapes. Bake at 425°F for 10 to 12 minutes. Serve warm.

APPLE AND RASPBERRY JAM

2 lb peeled, cored, sliced cooking apples
½ cup lemon juice
2/3 cup water
2 lb raspberries
4 lb sugar

In saucepan simmer apples with juice and water until tender. Add berries and sugar. Stir until sugar is dissolved. Boil to the setting point. Pour into warm sterilized jars and seal.

ORANGE GINGERBREAD

½ cup butter
½ cup sugar
½ cup molasses
1 beaten egg
1 orange, juice and grated rind
½ cup cold tea
1¾ cup flour
¾ tsp baking soda
1 tsp ginger

Cream butter, add sugar and mix until fluffy. Add molasses, egg, orange rind and juice. Beat well. Mix in tea and dry ingredients. Bake in loaf pan at 325°F for 40 minutes.

CINNAMON HOT CHOCOLATE

8 oz bittersweet chocolate, pieces
3 tbsp honey
½ tbsp cinnamon
¼ tsp nutmeg
4 cups milk

Put chocolate, honey, cinnamon and nutmeg in medium saucepan over very low heat. As chocolate melts, stir constantly to blend mixture. Slowly stir in milk. Increase heat and bring to boil, stirring continuously. Then immediately reduce heat and with wire whisk or an egg beater, carefully and vigorously beat the mixture until frothy. Pour into heated mugs. Serves 4

KENEALLY MANOR BED AND BREAKFAST

8 Patrick Street
Carbonear, NF A0A 1T0
(709) 596-1221
No. 6 on map, page 6

Keneally Manor, built in 1839 by the Keneally family from Ireland, remains an important part of our shipping heritage. Original architecture and antique furnishings create the ambience for the display of unique Newfoundland artwork, coins, stamps and trinkets found during restoration. Make yourself at home... relax on the settee in the private parlour and write postcards to your friends.

A town with almost four centuries of history is bound to have many old seafaring tales. Ask about the true love and romance legend of the swashbuckling captain and his Irish princess.

Now, get ready for fun! Horseback riding, scuba diving, trout fishing, historical sites and walking tours. Don't miss the excitement at their annual folk festival, bringing together local musicians and storytellers from all over the province.

Stop by the manor's gift shop. Your hostess, Janice Green, enjoys meeting people and will make you feel at home.

Keneally Manor awaits!

KENEALLY PARTRIDGEBERRY BREAD

2 cups flour
1½ tsp baking powder
1 cup sugar
½ tsp baking soda
¼ cup margarine
1 beaten egg
¾ cup orange juice
1 tbsp grated orange rind
½ cup chopped nuts
2 cups partridgeberries

Combine all dry ingredients in a bowl. Cut in margarine. Add beaten egg, orange juice and rind. Blend well. Fold in nuts and berries. Spoon into a greased loaf pan. Bake 50 to 60 minutes at 350°F. Check with toothpick for doneness.

One of the manor's special home made breads. Great at breakfast, brunch or anytime!

BANANA MILK

1 ripe medium banana
¾ cup milk
1 tbsp wheat germ
2 tsp honey
¼ tsp cinnamon

Overnight freeze peeled banana in airtight plastic bag. Puree ingredients in blender; pour in glasses. Serves 1-2

ORANGE SPARKLER

1½ cups orange juice
½ cup ginger ale

Pour juice in glasses. Stir in ginger ale. Serves 2

SUNSHINE SMOOTHIE

4 cups orange juice
1 banana

Whip banana in blender until smooth. Add juice and whip a few more seconds. Pour over ice. Serves 4-6.

RASPBERRY YOGURT SHAKE

1 cup plain yogurt
2 cups fresh or frozen raspberries or blueberries
½ cup sugar
1 tsp vanilla
1 tbsp vegetable oil
1/8 tsp salt
1 cup low-fat milk

Spin ingredients for 30 seconds in blender or until texture is consistent. Pour in glasses. Serves 4.

BRUNCH

Surprise your brunch guests with a tasty serving of cod or moose, sweet breads, cookies and a special tea or coffee. And why not dessert? After all, what better way to make a lasting impression. Be creative!

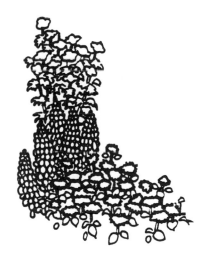

JUICE ON THE ROCKS

1 fully ripe tomato
½ cup clam juice
2 tbsp lemon juice
2 shakes tabasco sauce
½ cup cucumber slices

Blend all ingredients together for 10 seconds.
Serve over ice.

PASTA BRUNCH

4 cups cooked spaghetti or spiral noodles
4 tbsp unsalted butter
2 medium garlic cloves, finely chopped
8 well beaten eggs
½ cup parmesan cheese (divided)
3 tbsp chopped parsley
Fresh ground black pepper to taste

Melt butter in large fry pan, add cloves and simmer, 3 to 4 minutes. Drain pasta thoroughly, toss in butter. Add eggs and half the cheese. Increase heat slightly, and cook mixture. Stir until eggs are thick and have formed curds that cling to pasta. Stir in parsley. Transfer pasta to individual serving bowls. Sprinkle with remaining cheese and pepper to taste. Serves 4

GRAPEFRUIT SHRIMP SALAD

1 packet unflavoured gelatin
1 tsp sugar
½ cup cold water
1 cup unsweetened grapefruit juice
1 tbsp lemon juice
1 cup shrimp - finely chopped
1 cup grapefruit sections
½ cup chopped cucumber

Mix gelatin and sugar in sauce pan, add water. Cook over low heat, stirring until gelatin softens. In bowl, combine gelatin and juices. Refrigerate until consistency of unbeaten egg white. Mix remaining ingredients into gelatin mixture. Refrigerate until firm.

TOMATO BURGER CHOWDER

1½ lbs ground beef
1 finely chopped onion
1 28-oz can whole tomatoes
2 cups water
3 cans beef consumé
1 can tomato soup
4 diced carrots
1 bay leaf
3 diced celery sticks
Pepper, parsley, thyme to taste
8 tbsp cooking rice

Brown meat and onions. Drain well. In large pot mix together all ingredients. Cover and simmer 2 to 4 hours. Serves 8 to 10

CARMANVILLE OLDE INN

P. O. Box 16
Carmanville, NF
A0G 1N0
(709) 534-2544/2825
No. 15 on map, page 6

Have you ever seen a "Victrola"? Well, come to the Carmanville Olde Inn, only two minutes off the Gander Loop Highway, and you will see this rare antique. Dating back to the late 1800's, this authentic hand wound gramophone can still play their old collection of long-playing records that give you a unique magical sound. Requests anyone? The old family home has many other personal and sentimental heirlooms too. Great home cooking, warm hospitality... a great combination.

During your stay... Visit the shipwreck of "Ahern Trader" or go whale watching. Spot giant icebergs or picnic on the beautiful coastal beaches. Salmon fish or explore quiet walking trails. Pick berries to take home. Maybe tour Twillingate for the day. In winter you can enjoy winter carnival, cross-country skiing and ocean ice skating.

Carmanville gained prominence in the songs " Island of Newfoundland" and "Aunt Martha's Sheep". There's also a story about 6 men and a horse lost at sea in 1929 that is worth hearing.

Year-round fun for everyone!

COASTAL CLAM CHOWDER

½ lb bacon
1 large diced Spanish onion
¼ to ½ cup flour
2 tins baby clams and juice
4 tins clam nectar or 3 cups water
5 large diced celery stalks
5 large cubed potatoes
1 diced green pepper
Salt to taste
Pepper *(secret ingredient, so use lots)*
1½ tins evaporated milk

Crisp fry bacon in large saucepan, then dice it into small pieces. Cover and add onion to fry on simmer heat for 15 to 20 minutes. Stir in flour to absorb bacon fat. Add clams, water and/or nectar and slowly bring to a boil. Add celery, potatoes, green pepper, salt and pepper. Simmer for 10 to 15 minutes until the vegetables are cooked. Remove pot from heat. Stir in milk to cool chowder, but do not boil because milk will curdle.

Joan cautions, the milk must be put in last. If it boils, the chowder will be spoiled. So, be patient, the reward is worth it!

PEA SOUP and DOUGHBOYS

1 lb salt meat, spare rib or ham bone
2 cups split peas
6 cups water
1 chopped onion
1 cup diced celery
1 cup diced potato
1 small diced turnip
1 diced parsnip
3 diced carrots

SOUP: Soak salt meat and peas overnight in water, then drain it off. Add water and onion to meat and peas, simmer gently for 3 hours. Add more water as soup cooks, depending on preference for thick or thin soup. About 20 minutes before serving, add vegetables. Serve with doughboys.

¼ cup butter
1½ cup flour
3 tsp baking powder
½ tsp salt
½ to ¾ cup milk or water

DOUGHBOYS: Cut butter into small pieces in dry ingredients. Add milk gradually to make a soft dough. Drop by teaspoon into soup. Cover pot tightly and cook for 15 minutes. Don't peek until done.

POTATO au GRATIN

2 tbsp margarine
¼ cup chopped onion
2 tbsp flour
¾ tsp salt
¼ tsp dry mustard
1/8 tsp pepper
1 cup milk
½ tsp worchestershire sauce
¾ cup shredded cheese (divided)
4 medium size potatoes, sliced thin

Grease shallow dish, melt butter over low heat, add onion. Cook 2 to 3 minutes. In a jar, shake flour, salt, mustard, pepper and milk together. Add to melted margarine and onion. Stir until thickened. Add worchestershire sauce and ½ cup cheese. Stir until melted. Add potatoes. Sprinkle top with remaining cheese. Bake at 350°F for 30 minutes.

BEET and CABBAGE SALAD

2 cups shredded cabbage
1½ cups diced beet
½ cup green peas
1 apple, cubed
Mayonnaise

Mix cabbage and beet and let stand for an hour or so. Add peas and apple. Add mayonnaise as needed. Keep refrigerated until served.

PARKSIDE INN

P. O. Box 132
Port Rexton, NF A0C 2H0
(709) 464-2151
No. 11 on map, page 6

"Just like visiting one of my daughters," wrote a visitor about Christine, owner of Parkside Inn, Port Rexton. Comfortable rooms, licensed dining room, and lounge with local entertainment. Spend a quiet evening or mingle on the patio deck and BBQ stuffed salmon or cod. Request home cooked meals, and that's what you'll get - terrific!

Take Smoke Alley Trail and hike or cross-country ski from the front door. Drive to nearby Trinity, an historic community with churches, museums, craft shops, even a blacksmith shop. Stop in the heritage tea rooms at the Eriksen/Batson House. Spend the afternoon with your family on the Trinity Loop or take a scenic boat tour to Fox Island and Horse Chops to look for whales and icebergs. Want to go cod jigging? There's salmon and trout fishing too, or tour the arctic char fish farm. From its central location on the Discovery Trail tourist route, you can easily day trip to Bonavista and the national park. In winter, downhill ski at White Hills near Clarenville, or get in the swing of summer on the Twin Rivers golf course.

A convenient location and friendly hospitality!

SAVOURY SCALLOP BAKE

½ cup flour
½ tsp salt
Pinch of pepper
1 tsp Newfoundland savory
1 pound scallops
1 tbsp cream or whole milk
1 tsp butter
Fine dry bread crumbs

Mix flour, salt, pepper and savory together. Dip scallops in this mixture and divide them in four greased scallop shells or individual dishes. In a bowl, combine cream with melted butter. Spoon mixture over scallops. Sprinkle with bread crumbs. Bake for 20 minutes in preheated oven set at 450°F.

Newfoundland savory, a course herbal seasoning, is the key ingredient in this recipe. When it comes out of the hot oven, Christine adds a few drops of lemon for added flavour. Serve with your favourite salad or take it over to a friend's house as a buffet casserole. Simple and easy to make!

LOBSTER N' BUTTER

Use the ocean's salt water if possible. Otherwise, add 4 tbsp salt to fresh water in large pot. Bring to a boil, then add live lobsters. Make sure the lobsters are covered with water. Boil water again for 20 minutes, drain off water and let lobsters cool. Dip in Lemon Butter and eat to your heart's content!

LEMON BUTTER: Melt ¼ cup butter and add 2 tsp lemon juice, mix well. Dip cooked hot lobster meat in butter.

ATLANTIC LOBSTER QUICHE

2 10-inch baked pie crusts
¾ lb fresh or tin lobster meat
2 cups grated Swiss cheese
2 tbsp minced green onion
4 beaten eggs
2 cups light cream
Salt and pepper to taste
1/8 tsp nutmeg (optional)
4 tbsp parmesan cheese

In pie shells, spread lobster meat, sprinkle cheese, then onion. Beat eggs in bowl and add cream. Stir in salt, pepper and nutmeg. Pour egg mixture over lobster in pie shells. Bake at 350°F for 25 to 30 minutes. Add parmesan cheese on top; broil until cheese slightly melts. Makes 2

CHEDDAR MUSSEL BAKE

4 lb mussels, cleaned and beards removed
Salt and pepper to taste
½ cup finely chopped onion
2 tbsp lemon juice
6 slices chopped bacon
1 cup grated old cheddar cheese

Rinse mussels well. Discard any that do not close when tapped. In large covered saucepan, cook them using a small amount of boiling water until the shells open, 6-8 minutes. Remove meat from shells and place in buttered baking dish. Season and sprinkle with onion and lemon. Cover with bacon and cheese. Bake at 375°F for 15 to 20 minutes or until bacon is cooked.

CAPLIN FRITTERS

1 1/3 cups flour
Dash salt, pepper and cayenne pepper
¾ cup milk
3 tsp oil
1 egg yolk
1 egg white stiffly beaten
2 cups caplin, cleaned, boned, cubed

Sift together flour, salt, pepper and cayenne. Combine milk, oil and egg yolk. Add this liquid to flour mixture, blend well. Let stand one hour. Fold in egg white. Heat oil to 375°F. Dip fish pieces in batter. Deep fry 3 to 4 minutes until golden, drain well. Makes 24

BROCCOLI and CORN CASSEROLE

1 can cream of mushroom soup
¼ cup mayonnaise
¼ cup sour cream
1 egg yolk
1 10-oz package frozen chopped broccoli,
    thawed and drained
1 10-oz package frozen whole corn,
    thawed and drained
1 cup shredded cheddar cheese
½ cup chopped onion
1/3 cup crumbled crackers
1 tsp melted margarine

Mix first four ingredients. Stir in broccoli, corn, cheese and onion. Spoon into greased shallow baking dish. Stir together crumbs and melted butter. Sprinkle over mixture. Bake for 30 to 35 minutes at 350°F. Serves 6 to 8

GLAZED CARROTS with ONIONS

6 medium carrots, sliced
1 large chopped onion
½ cup water
1 tsp salt
2 tbsp brown sugar
2 tbsp butter

Combine all ingredients in a pot. Cover and bake 60 minutes at 375°F. Remove cover a few minutes before end of baking time. Serves 8

VEGGIES in POTATO CUPS

3 cups mashed potatoes (about 6 potatoes)
¼ cup finely chopped onion
¼ cup shredded Swiss cheese
1 egg yolk
2 tbsp finely cut green onion
½ tsp salt
Pepper to taste
1½ cups broccoli, small pieces
1½ cups cubed carrots
¼ cup grated cheddar cheese (optional)

Mix together all ingredients, except broccoli, carrots and cheddar cheese. Divide mixture into large greased muffin pan (8 cups), patting evenly on bottom and up sides to form potato cups. Bake at 350°F for 30 to 35 minutes or until golden brown. Cool slightly. Loosen with knife, remove carefully. Meanwhile, steam carrots and broccoli until barely tender; drain well, and spoon into warm potato cups, sprinkle with cheddar cheese. Serves 8

CAULIFLOWER BROCCOLI with CURRY CHEESE

1 cup grated cheese or cheese whiz
1 tbsp milk
½ tsp curry powder
1 cup hot cooked broccoli, well drained
1 cup hot cooked cauliflower, well drained

Stir cheese, milk and curry in saucepan over low heat to melt. Pour over combined vegetables. Serves 4 to 6

PEACE COVE INN

Trinity East, NF
(Mail: P. O. Box 48
Paradise, NF A1L 1C4)
(709) 464-3738/781-2255
No. 10 on map, page 6

Originally owned by a local schooner captain... Peace Cove Inn is a restored turn of the century Newfoundland heritage home that perfectly combines comfort and tradition. It's modern facilities and restful accommodations retain the original charm and decor that compliment the traditional outport hospitality. Newfoundland cooking is a speciality... from Jiggs dinner to fine seafood. Breads, pies and desserts are prepared daily in their kitchens. Dinner by reservation, and lunch on request.

The ocean's playground is yours to experience when aboard their 46 foot pilothouse motorsailer. Icebergs, whales, seabirds, are possible sightings when the skipper plots his course for your Atlantic Adventure.

You can... Walk the quaint country paths or wander along the coastal trails. Visit the museum, churches and other historical sites in Trinity or tour the Bonavista Peninsula as a day trip.

Discover yesterday... today... at Peace Cove Inn.

PEACE COVE BAKED COD

4 tbsp melted margarine
3 lb fresh cod (or frozen fillets)
Salt and pepper to taste
1 finely chopped onion or green onion
4 strips of bacon

Preheat oven to 425°F. Put 2 tablespoons melted margarine in casserole dish that is large enough to hold the cod in a single layer. Place cod in dish. Add salt, pepper and onion. Sprinkle fish with remaining 2 tablespoons melted margarine. Arrange bacon strips on top of the fish. Bake uncovered approximately 15 minutes.

"The cod has a very pleasant smoked taste," advises Art, your host. It's quick and easy. What a treat to the palate!

CODFISH CAKES

2 chopped onions
2 cups cooked salt cod, deboned and flaked
6 to 8 cooked potatoes
3 cooked parsnips
1 tsp butter
Pepper to taste
1 well beaten egg
½ cup fine bread crumbs

Cook onions in small amount of water. Mash fish, potatoes, parsnips, and butter together. Add onions and its water. Season with pepper, add egg and combine well. Chill until cool and firm. Form 3-inch patty cakes, dip in crumbs. Fry them in pork fat drippings or vegetable oil for 2 to 3 minutes on each side. Turn once, until golden and crisp. Serves 6

CAULCANNON

Caulcannon, a Newfoundland tradition to celebrate the Fall vegetable harvest, is often served at supper on Halloween night. It is usually made from vegetables such as potato, carrot, cabbage, parsnip, turnip and onion. Many people use Jiggs Dinner leftovers.

Cook the vegetables you prefer, then put them though a potato ricer. Mix well, add a little butter and pepper for flavour if you like. For cold leftovers, however, heat the riced mixture. Spoon into plates and serve hot.

SAUCY COD on TOAST

6 pieces buttered toast
3 sliced hard-boiled eggs
1 cup cooked flaked cod
1 cup thin white sauce
6 slices crisp bacon

Layer toast with eggs, fish and cover with sauce. Garnish with bacon.

	Thin	*Medium*	*Thick*
Butter	1 tbsp	2 tbsp	3 tbsp
Flour	1 tbsp	2 tbsp	3 tbsp
Milk	1 cup	1 cup	1 cup

Salt and pepper to taste

SAUCE: Melt butter, add flour and mix well. Cook 1 minute, slowly add milk. Add salt, pepper, and boil 2 minutes. Pour over cod on toast.

TUNA SALAD BURGERS

1 7-oz can tuna
1 cup shredded cheese
3 chopped hard boiled eggs
2 tbsp finely chopped onion
2 tbsp sweet relish
½ cup mayonnaise or salad dressing

Mix all ingredients. Spread on hamburger bun halves. Heat oven to 375°F. Place in oven, remove when cheese is melted.

WHALEN'S HOSPITALITY HOME

P. O. Box 46
Branch, NF
A0B 1E0
(709) 338-2506
No. 7 on map, page 6

"Savour the flavour" is the motto of Whalen's Bed and Breakfast. A genuine welcome and friendly hospitality greets you at the door. Enjoy comfort and privacy in their large family home. Traditional meals are available on request. Rosemary's a great cook, so I would strongly consider this option.

Only a few minutes away, you will find the main fishing activities down at the "gut". Perhaps a local fisherman, in his Newfoundland-Irish accent will offer you tips on catching the huge sea trout or salmon in the river that runs throughout the tiny community.

Only a short drive away, visit the seabird ecological reserve where kittiwakes, razor-billed ducks, and gannets, impress nature lovers from all over the world. Take a picnic break on the beach to watch for whales and icebergs. In season there's partridgeberries, bakeapples, and blueberries for picking.

Bring your camera... your paint brush or whatever you like to capture our natural traditions!

FISHERMEN'S BREWIS

4 cakes hard bread
Fatback pork
2 large onions, chopped
Fresh cod
1 tsp salt

In a large pot, soak hard bread overnight in plenty of cold water. Drain off water the next morning and refill again. When ready to cook softened bread to make brewis, add salt to the water and bring to a boil. Immediately remove from heat and drain well. In separate pot, add water and boil fish. Drain fish. Make sure the skin and bones are removed. Add fish and bread together, chop well. In pan, fry out small pieces of fatback pork and onions. Pour this hot liquid and onions over chopped fish and brewis. Mix well together. Serves 4 to 6

Rosemary usually makes her brewis with fresh fish, however, if you use salt fish, be sure to soak it in water overnight to remove the salt. Drain and cook the fish the next day the same as the fresh cod in this recipe.

Hard bread cakes, fatback pork, and cod - three traditional ingredients in one dish. You'll love it!

RIVER MUFFINS

1 cup salmon, cooked and flaked
¼ cup shredded old cheddar cheese
1/3 cup sour cream
¼ cup celery, finely chopped
1½ cups flour
2 tbsp sugar
2 tsp baking powder
½ tsp salt
¼ tsp thyme
1 egg, slightly beaten
¾ cup milk
1/3 cup oil

Combine salmon, cheese, sour cream, celery and set aside. In a bowl, mix dry ingredients. Make a well in centre. Using another bowl, beat egg, milk and oil. Add to dry ingredients, stirring to moisten. Fill greased muffin cups and top with 1 tbsp of the salmon mixture. Bake 375°F for 20 minutes. Serve warm. *Substitute lobster or shrimp.*

SALMON NUTTY FRUIT SALAD

1 lb fresh drained, cooked salmon (or tinned salmon)
1 tbsp lemon juice
2 oranges, peeled, sectioned, chunked
1 sliced banana
¼ cup blanched almonds, split and roasted
3 cups lettuce, small pieces
1 unpeeled red apple

Break salmon into small pieces and sprinkle with lemon juice. Combine fruit, add salmon, almonds, and lettuce, toss lightly. Serve with favourite fruit salad dressing. Serves 6

SALMON FRENCH TOAST

3¾ oz can of salmon or tuna
½ cup liquid (salmon juice plus water)
1½ tbsp mayonnaise
1 tsp chopped parsley (optional)
1 tsp chopped onion
¼ tsp salt
Dash of pepper
4 slices whole wheat or white bread
1 egg well beaten
2 tbsp skim milk powder

Drain salmon and save juice. Flake salmon and mix with mayonnaise, parsley, onion and seasonings. Spread on two slices of bread and top with the other two. Combine egg, salmon liquid and milk powder in shallow dish. Dip sandwiches into this mixture. Brown both sides in frying pan, and serve with fruit. Serves 2

RICE and CARROT CASSEROLE

1 cup instant rice or 2 cups cooked rice
2 cups grated carrots
3 beaten eggs
3 cups milk
¼ tsp nutmeg
2 tbsp sugar
1 tsp salt

Mix all ingredients together. Bake at 350°F for 75 minutes. Serves 4 to 6

THE "OLDE HOUSE" BED AND BREAKFAST

9 American Drive
St. Anthony, NF A0K 4S0
(709) 454-3794/454-0005
No. 18 on map, page 6

Tall balsam trees outline the walkway leading to the front steps of The "Olde House" Bed and Breakfast, located in St. Anthony on the Viking Trail. From the veranda get a full view of the peaceful little harbour. This large traditional family home has everything: swings in the garden, a cozy sitting room with logs on the fire, a large brass bed, an old-fashioned bathtub, a special craft corner, even the daily newspaper. A full breakfast or a special requested meal, you can be sure the taste of Pauline's home cooking will be delicious.

A must do and see is the Jordi Bonet Murals in the main lobby of the Curtis Memorial Hospital - exceptional eskimo art, well worth the time. Next, visit the Grenfell House Museum which tells the story of the man they called "the fishermen's doctor". Then on to L'Anse aux Meadows with its reconstructed 1000 year old Viking settlement of sod houses.

The annual Cod Festival and Barsok Folk Festival promise fascinating activities, lively music and wholesome fun.

Treat yourself to a terrific place along the Viking Trail!

LABRADOR SALMON with SMOKED OYSTER DRESSING

1½ to 2 cups cooked brown rice
1 chopped onion
½ chopped green pepper
1 chopped celery stalk
6 thinly sliced mushrooms
1 can smoked oysters (chop, reserve oil)
1 crushed clove garlic
1 tbsp chopped parsley
½ tsp ginger
Salt and pepper

DRESSING: Combine the above ingredients and mix well.

4 to 5 pounds whole salmon, cleaned
1 thinly sliced lemon

SALMON: Stuff salmon with oyster dressing. Place fish on foil and garnish with overlapping slices of lemon. Wrap securely in two layers of foil. Bake for 1 hour at 350°F. Serves 6 to 8

Pauline's catering business clients love this special recipe. Salmon and oysters - oceans of flavour! What a terrific combination!

RAINBOW TROUT in WINE

6 fresh rainbow trout (1 lb each)
¾ cup white wine
¼ tsp rosemary
¼ tsp dill seeds
½ tsp salt

Wash trout in salted, cold water. Pat dry. Place in large frying pan with wine and seasonings. Bring to boil, reduce heat and simmer gently for 20 minutes, turning once. Remove fish from liquid, let cool, then remove skin and bones. Serves 6

LEMONY THYME CHICKEN

1 tbsp butter or margarine
2 tbsp vegetable oil
3½ lbs cut up chicken or rabbit
½ cup lemon juice
6 green onions, finely chopped
½ tsp salt
½ tsp thyme
Pinch of pepper

In heavy saucepan, heat butter and oil. Add chicken and cook until browned. Stir in remaining ingredients. Bring to a boil, cover, reduce heat and simmer 1 hour or until tender.

ROAST CARIBOU RIBS

4 tbsp flour
¼ tsp pepper (or to taste)
Pinch of garlic powder
¼ tsp dry mustard
6 short ribs, 4-inch lengths
2 medium onions, chopped
3 tbsp bacon fat
1 tbsp vinegar
½ cup chopped celery
1 cup water
1 tsp salt
¼ cup dry red wine
3 tbsp cornstarch
1 tbsp worchestershire sauce

Mix first 4 ingredients. Rub flour mixture into ribs and sear in hot fry pan. Place ribs in roast pan. Add onions to fat in fry pan and cook until soft. Add other ingredients, bring to a bubble only. Pour over ribs, cover, bake at 350°F for 1 hour.

BROILED BRUNCH TENDERLOIN

1½ tsp unsalted butter, softened
1 tbsp worchestershire sauce
Salt and freshly ground black pepper
6 beef tenderloin steaks

Mash butter with sauce, season to taste. Spread butter evenly on both sides of steak. When broiler is hot, place steaks on broiler tray. Cook 2-inches from heat for 3 to 4 minutes per side for medium rare. Serves 6

SEASIDE LODGE BED AND BREAKFAST

341 Main Street
Lewisporte, NF A0G 3A0
(709) 535-6305
No. 16 on map, page 6

Cruise boats! Passenger boats! Freight ships! See them all in the busy harbour of Lewisporte. Enjoy all this and more when you stay at the Seaside Lodge Bed and Breakfast, only minutes off the main highway. A great place to relax is on the patio deck overlooking the bay or take a leisurely stroll along the wharf closeby. Perhaps you'd like to lounge in front of the fire with a cup of tea and nibble on one of Naomi's homemade muffins.

Why not spend a day on the water and jig a cod. Then slip into a sheltered little cove to cook it for supper. Fun for the whole family. In the park there are picnic areas, a beach, and nature trails. You can tour the historical train and visit the craft shop in the antique museum. Neighboring folks sell their fresh vegetables in season. Wintertime, bring your skis and head out on the cross country trails.

At the Annual Mussel Bed Soiree in July, get your foot stomping and learn the Newfie shuffle. If you would like to attend the lobster boils and salmon festivals in the surrounding communities, bus tours are available.

Friendly hospitality year round!

TENDER MOOSE STEW

3 to 4 pounds moose (roast section)
1 large onion
4 medium carrots
2 medium turnip
6 to 8 medium potatoes
1 tsp salt
½ tsp pepper (or to taste)
1 tsp Newfoundland savory
½ tsp gravy browning
shortening
4 cups water

THICKENING PASTE: Put 1 cup cold water and 4 tbsp flour in bottle with lid, and shake to mix paste for stew.

STEW: Cut meat in ½-inch chunks. Brown in shortening in fry pan or deep dish on medium heat for approximately 30 minutes. Reduce to low temperature for the next 30 minutes. Dice vegetables and add with seasonings to meat. Add water and let simmer for 30 minutes. Stir in gravy browning and above prepared white thickening paste. Let bubble until it thickens into a gravy.   Serve 4 to 6

"The longer it cooks, the better the taste," says Naomi. Get out the butter and hot fresh home made buns. Dig in before it's all gone!

BOLONEY CUPS

Whole bologna (slice ½-inch thick)
Potatoes
Butter, pepper and milk (to own taste)
Grated cheese

Slice bologna ½-inch thick, remove skin and boil for 2 to 3 minutes until slices curl up like cups. Cook potatoes and mash with butter, pepper and milk. Fill cups with mashed potatoes and bake at 350°F until browned, about 5 minutes. Top with cheese and serve.

ORANGE RHUBARB PORK CHOPS

4 pork chops
1/3 cup flour
1½ tsp salt
¼ tsp pepper
1 1/3 cup chopped rhubarb
1/3 cup brown sugar
¼ tsp cloves
1 medium onion, sliced
1 orange, peeled and thinly sliced
½ cup chopped celery
1/3 cup water

Cut fat off pork chops. In a bowl, combine flour, salt, pepper and roll pork chops in mixture. Brown in frying pan. Place chops in baking dish. Toss rhubarb in sugar and cloves mixture. Top chops with onion, orange and celery. Sprinkle rhubarb and water over top. Cover with foil and bake at 375°F for 1 hour.

JIGGS DINNER and PEAS PUDDING

2 lb salt beef (corned beef) or salt spareribs
1 cup yellow split peas
1 medium turnip, peeled, cubed
6 carrots
6 to 8 medium potatoes
1 medium cabbage, cut in wedges
Butter and pepper to taste

DINNER: Soak meat in cold water overnight. Drain and place in large pot. Tie peas in cloth bag, leaving room to expand, and put bag in pot with beef. Cover with fresh water, bring to a boil, then cover, simmer for 2 to 3 hours. Add vegetables to pot in the following order: turnip, carrots, potatoes and cabbage, allowing 15 minutes between each addition. Cook until potatoes are tender. Serves 6 to 8

PUDDING: Remove pudding from bag, mash in bowl with butter and pepper. Arrange vegetables and meat on plate, spoon stock (pot liquor) from the pot over entire dinner. *Liquid may be used to make gravy for moose, beef or chicken.* Serves 6 to 8

EASY TURNIP BAKE

2 eggs, separated
3 tbsp milk
Salt and pepper to taste
2 cups cooked turnip, mashed

Beat egg yolks and milk. Add salt, pepper and turnip. Mix thoroughly. Beat egg whites until stiff peaks form. Fold turnip mixture into beaten egg whites. Bake for 30 minutes at 350°F.

FIGGY DUFF

3 cups bread crumbs
1 cup raisins
½ cup brown sugar
Dash of salt
1 tsp ginger
1 tsp allspice
1 tsp cinnamon
¼ cup melted butter
3 tbsp molasses
1 tsp baking soda
1 tbsp hot water
½ cup flour

Combine crumbs, raisins, sugar, salt and spices. Add melted butter, molasses, and baking soda which has been dissolved in water. Add flour and combine well. Pour into a dampened pudding bag. Steam 1½ hours. *Pudding often served with Jiggs Dinner.*

CHEDDAR CHEESE BREAD

3 cups flour
4 tsp baking powder
½ tsp salt
1½ cups grated cheddar cheese
1½ cups milk
2 tbsp margarine or butter

Combine flour, baking powder, salt and cheese in large bowl. Stir thoroughly. Add milk and melted margarine. Stir to form soft dough. Put in greased loaf pan. Bake at 400°F for 35 to 40 minutes. Makes 1 loaf.

IRISH BRAN BREAD

½ cup corn meal
1 cup bran
3 cups whole wheat flour
½ cup white flour
¾ tsp salt
1½ tsp baking soda
1½ tsp cream of tartar
2 cups buttermilk

Mix corn meal, bran, and flour. Add remaining dry ingredients. Mix thoroughly. Make a well in dry ingredients and add buttermilk all at once. Stir to mix. Add more flour if too sticky. Shape dough with floured hands and press into greased 9 x 5-inch loaf pan. Bake at 400°F for about 60 minutes. Cool in pan 10 minutes, then put on rack to finish cooling. Makes 1 loaf

FOGGY BAKEAPPLE SOUP

3 cups orange juice
3 cups low fat yogurt
2 tbsp lime or lemon juice
3 cups bakeapple berries
Garnish with cinnamon or nutmeg

Whisk together orange juice and yogurt. Add lime juice. Cover and chill until serving. When ready to serve, place about ½ cup berries in each bowl, ladle soup on top. Garnish. Serves 4 *Try other frozen or fresh berries. Great as a dessert, beverage, appetizer or morning meal.*

CLUETT'S HOSPITALITY HOME

17 Church Street
Garnish, NF
A0E 1T0
(709) 826-2665
No. 8 on map, page 6

As you drive towards Cluett's Bed and Breakfast in Garnish, Fortune Bay, you can't help, but admire the immensity of the ocean stretching before you. Fresh air and green, blue water gently foaming over the grey pebble stone beach nearby. Peaceful and quiet, with coastline beauty where you can play in the sun... picnic on the beach... and splash in the ocean.

Next to a church which overlooks the ocean, Bertha's white house is easy to find... just ask anyone. She enjoys meeting guests all year round and they fancy her fresh baked goodies.

There's lots to do... nature trails, bird watching, boating trips to look for whales, or go cod jigging! Tour the 90 year old lighthouse! Only 30 minutes away, you can take the ferry to the island of St. Pierre for the day and experience a little part of France.

The annual bakeapple festival held in August usually has music and dancing into the wee hours of the morning.

Travelling alone or with friends, you'll get sincere hospitality!

STEAMED MOLASSES PUDDING and SAUCE

¼ cup melted butter
3 tbsp sugar
¼ cup molasses
1 tsp cinnamon
½ tsp allspice
¼ cup boiling water
½ tsp baking soda
¾ cup flour
½ cup raisins or blueberries

PUDDING: Mix butter, sugar and molasses. Add cinnamon, allspice and stir well. Combine boiling water and soda. Mix all together. Add flour, then raisins or berries last. Pour into greased mold (1 quart) and tie waxed paper loosely over top. Place mold on rack in bottom of deep pot. Pour in boiling water to half the depth of mold. Cover and allow to steam one hour. Replenish the water if necessary, with more boiling water to keep original level. Serve hot with this sauce. Serves 4

1 cup brown sugar
1 tbsp butter
2 tsp flour
2 cups boiling water

SAUCE: Mix all ingredients. Add water until it thickens. Pour over pudding.

Steamed pudding is a favourite dessert in Newfoundland, especially one made with molasses!

RAISIN MOLASSES BREAD

1 package active dry yeast
1 tsp sugar
½ cup lukewarm water
2½ cups fresh milk
1½ tsp salt
¼ cup margarine
½ cup cooking molasses
6 to 7 cups flour
2 tsp cinnamon
1 tsp mace
1 tsp cloves
3 to 4 cups raisins

Dissolve yeast in lukewarm sugared water. Wait 10 to 15 minutes for yeast to bubble. In saucepan, heat milk, salt, and melt butter. Cool to lukewarm. In large bowl combine molasses, yeast mixture, 3 cups flour, spices and raisins. Beat 2 to 3 minutes. Continue adding flour to make moist soft dough. Knead on clean flat surface for about 10 minutes until dough becomes smooth and elastic. Add more flour if dough is still sticky. Move to greased bowl, put in warm place to double in size, about 1½ to 2 hours. Divide dough in half and shape in two loafs. Place in greased 9 x 5 loaf pans and let rise again until doubled, about 1 to 2 hours. Bake at 375°F for 1 hour, until brown.

POWDERED MILK BREAD

6 cups white flour
1 package yeast
½ cup warm water
1 cup shortening
½ cup sugar
1 cup powdered milk
½ cup cold water
1 tbsp salt

Sift flour in large bowl. Dissolve yeast and 1 tsp sugar in warm water. Stir with fork and let rise. In another bowl add salt, remaining sugar and soft shortening; rub together. Dissolve powdered milk in cold water. Stir dry mixture with hands and make a well in the flour. Add milk and shortening mixture and work with hands until all the flour is used. Knead for 5 minutes. Cover and let rise until double in bulk. Keep warm with blanket (or heating pad set on "low" placed under bowl), approximate 1 hour. Then knead and let rise again to double in bulk. Put in warm, greased loaf pans. Bake at 300°F for 40 minutes. Makes 4 loafs

DOGBERRY and APPLE JELLY

24 apples, sliced only
1 qt dogberries
¾ cup sugar for each cup of juice

Do not peel or core apples. Cover apples and berries with cold water. Cook until tender about 20 minutes. Strain through a cheese cloth or jelly bag. Measure juice and add sugar for each cup of juice. Boil until drop of juice jells. Pour into sterilized jars and seal.

RIVERSIDE LODGE (TOURIST HOME)

Site 3, Box 9
Trouty, Trinity Bay
NF A0C 2S0
(709) 464-3780/3578
No. 12 on map, page 6

Hidden in a tiny fishing village, just off the Discovery Trail Highway, you will find the Riverside Lodge (Tourist Home). It borders a small, but fast running salmon river that winds through the little community and down to the sea. Smell the sweet scent of the spruce forest and salt of the ocean brine, listen to the sounds of silence... yes, nature is that close. What a way to relax and enjoy yourself!

Warm hospitality and great home cooking... specialities are cod and salmon dinners.

Want to go to sea? Squid jigging and "hand line" cod jigging boat trips are easily arranged. There's special tours in the area for whale watching, perhaps you will see an iceberg. Nearby visit a railway museum and amusement train park, then hike the trails at Kerly's Harbour. The area is a painter's paradise... beautiful coastal scenery everywhere. Only a few minutes away, you can drive to the historical sites of Trinity, then, the next morning do a day trip to see the Bonavista lighthouse.

A terrific place in the country to relax!

PARTRIDGEBERRY PUDDING and SAUCE

½ cup butter
½ cup sugar
1 egg
1½ cups partridgeberries
2 cups flour
2 tsp baking powder
Pinch of salt
1 cup milk
½ tsp vanilla

PUDDING: Cream butter and sugar together. Add egg. Toss partridgeberries in ¼ cup flour and set aside. Sift remaining dry ingredients into egg mixture. Stir milk and vanilla together and mix into batter. Add berries and mix lightly. Bake at 350°F for 30 minutes, or until golden.

1 envelope custard powder
¼ cup water
1¾ cup water
½ tsp butter
1 cup brown sugar, lightly packed

SAUCE: Dissolve custard powder in water. Mix together all the ingredients. Cook over medium heat until sauce thickens. Serve over pudding. Serves 10 to 12

Annette varies her recipe using blueberries, and often, makes the pudding without berries to serve as a cottage pudding. Delicious!

STRAWBERRY RHUBARB and APPLE STEW

1 orange, grated rind and juice
2 cups fresh or frozen rhubarb
1 large apple
1 cup water
¼ cup sugar
2 cups fresh strawberries
½ cup low-fat plain yogurt
2 tbsp packed brown sugar

Cut rhubarb into 1-inch lengths. Peel, core and thinly slice apple. In saucepan, combine orange rind and juice, rhubarb, apple, water and sugar. Cover and bring to a boil. Reduce heat and simmer 10 minutes or until fruit is tender, stirring occasionally. Remove from heat and stir in strawberries. Add more sugar to taste. Serve warm. Top each serving with a spoonful of yogurt and sprinkle with brown sugar. Serves 8 *Raisins or apricots may be added during cooking, or after cooking, top with fresh fruit.*

SCREECH BAKEAPPLE SYLLABUB

2½ cups whipped cream
4 tbsp sugar
¾ cup bakeappples
½ cup screech (rum)
Garnish with chocolate

Combine cream and sugar. Whip until peaks form. Fold in bakeapples and screech slowly. Spoon mixture into individual dessert dishes and garnish with chocolate. Serves 4 *Screech is a very dark Newfoundland rum.*

ENGLISH SUMMER PUDDING

10 slices bread, crusts removed
Milk
Sugar
Berries - blueberries, red currants, raspberries,
       or sweet fruit combination

Dip bread in milk and line sides and bottom of greased baking dish with them. Sprinkle with a little sugar and cook for 3 to 4 minutes at 350°F. Remove from oven and put fruit and its juice in centre of baking dish. Cover top with bread. Cover baking dish with something tight fitting and heavy (to weigh it down). Let cool overnight. To serve, remove cover and turn upside down. *Great with whipped or fresh cream.*

BLANC MANGE

2 tbsp flour
A little water
2 cups milk
2 tsp vanilla
Sugar to taste

Make smooth thickening paste of flour and water. In saucepan on low heat, bring milk, vanilla and sugar to a boil. Remove from heat and add thickening. (May not need to add all the thickening to the milk mixture.) Stir and pour into bowl to set and cool. Great over jelly, stewed prunes, or other fruit.

MARY'S BED AND BREAKFAST

Little Port Road
Lark Harbour
(Mail: P. O. Box 231
Corner Brook, NF
A2H 6C9)
(709) 681-2210
or 789-3642
No. 20 on map, page 6

Jigging cod in the emerald blue waters around the Bay of Islands was customary for the Basque fishermen in the 1600's. Today, while visiting Mary's Bed and Breakfast in Lark Harbour, you can can still watch the in-shore fishermen unloading their fish, and sometimes buy their "catch" at the end of the day. The scenic coastal drive, offset by the grandeur of the Blow Me Down Mountains and the golden sands of the tiny secluded islands, is a photographer's delight.

There's lots to do for the adventurer, or the slower pace traveller. Row a dory around Bottle Cove, scuba dive and explore the caverns for lost treasure, play volleyball on the beach, swim in the ocean, or picnic and hike along the cliffs.

The city, only 30 minutes away, offers shopping and lively night spots to dance the night away.

You will not want to miss the fun at the annual Strawberry Festival in late July.

Natural beauty and intuitive hospitality!

SQUASHBERRY PUDDING and SAUCE

1½ cups flour
1 cup sugar
2 eggs
1/3 cup margarine
½ cup milk
1 cup squashberries
1 tsp vanilla
2 tsp baking powder

PUDDING: Cream margarine, sugar and eggs. Mix dry ingredients together, then add to creamed mixture. Stir by hand until blended, then gently stir in berries. Pour in greased loaf pans. Bake at 350°F for 45 to 60 minutes.

2 tsp butter
½ cup brown sugar
¼ tsp salt
1 cup water
1 tsp vanilla

SAUCE: Boil and thicken with cornstarch. Add water and serve hot over pudding.

Mary also makes her pudding with blueberries. However, she suggests not using berries such as raspberries, strawberries and bakeapples because they will make the pudding too soggy.

Squashberries, clear orange-red fruit that ripen late in August, also make great jelly.

Treat yourself!

RAISIN STUFFED APPLES

Small apples or pears, one for each person
Raisins and raspberry jam mixed together
1 unbaked pie pastry for every three apples
Cinnamon
Sugar

Core each apple from the top. Do not go all the way through, but slice a 1-inch pocket across. Spoon jam into pocket. Cut pie pastry into 4 pieces. Cover with ¼ pie pastry rolled thin. Use ¼ of pastry to fill in any open areas. Sprinkle with a mixture of sugar and cinnamon. Bake at 375°F for 30 minutes.

MAPLE BLUEBERRY GRUNT

½ cup water
½ cup sugar
2 tbsp maple syrup
1 qt blueberries
1½ cups flour
2 tsp baking powder
½ tsp salt
2 tsp sugar
1 tbsp butter
2/3 cup milk
Fresh cream or whipping cream for topping

Boil water and sugar to make syrup, add maple syrup and heat a few minutes more. Add blueberries and boil to make sauce. Sift dry ingredients and cut in butter. Add enough milk to make a soft dough, then drop one tablespoon at a time into boiling sauce when berries are soft. Cover tightly and cook rapidly for 15 minutes (no peeking), top with cream. Serves 5 to 6

EASY RHUBARB PIE

1 egg
1 cup sugar
3 tbsp flour
¾ tsp mixed spices (nutmeg and cinnamon)
2 cups cut rhubarb
Unbaked pie pastry for top and bottom

Beat egg well. Add sugar, flour and spices. Blend and add rhubarb. Pour mixture in pastry pie shell and top with pastry. Bake at 375°F, until rhubarb is tender.

SWEET TART PASTRY

½ cup butter
¾ cup brown sugar
2 egg yolks
1½ cups sifted flour
1 tsp baking powder
Pinch of salt

Cream butter, sugar and yolks until smooth. Add sifted dry ingredients and blend well. Pat mixture into tart pans, reserving some to use as topping if desired. Fill 2/3 full with filling. For top, roll reserved dough to 1/8-inch thickness and cut to cover each tart. Press edges together and prick top to allow steam to escape. Bake at 400°F for 15 to 18 minutes. Makes 20

PINSENT'S BED AND BREAKFAST

17 Church Street
Eastport, NF A0G 1Z0
(709) 677-3021
No. 13 on map, page 6

In 1903, farmer and fisherman, Adam Bradley built a beautiful saltbox style home. Today, owned by a horseman and painter, Pinsent's Bed and Breakfast preserves and reflect its heritage. Sweet fragrances of roses and lilacs in the garden surround their charmingly decorated home. A private collection of Walt's work is proudly displayed throughout the house. His art studio is nearby, perhaps you'll even get a chance to tour it.

While visiting the area you can... Catch caplin rolling at Sandy Cove. Relax on beautiful Eastport Beach. Visit Salvage community museum. Why not take a horseback tour offering daily trail or overnight camp rides. Ogle an eagle as you hike... fish for trout at sunset... catch a whale on film, or just listen to nature.

At the local summer music festival, you can learn to dance the "jig" in no time. When winter spreads her white blanket, then you can cross-country or downhill ski only an hour's drive from town.

A "home away from home"!

COUNTRY BLUEBERRY PIE

4 cups blueberries (fresh or frozen)
1 cup white sugar
6 tbsp corn starch
1 baked 9-inch pie crust
Whipping topping or fresh cream

Crush 2 cups of blueberries and simmer 5 minutes, stirring constantly. Mix sugar and corn starch together. Add to cooked berries. Stir until thicken. Remove from heat and add the remaining 2 cups blueberries. *Frozen berries will cool the sauce quickly.* Pour in baked pie shell. Let it set 2 hours. Decorate top of pie with whipped topping. Makes one terrific pie or 24 mouth-watering tarts.

Lillian's secret - After the hot sauce is cooked, add the uncooked berries. These whole blueberries will help cool the sauce, but stay plump and juicy.

Mouth-watering!

LEMON RUM BANANAS

2 tbsp lemon juice
½ cup white rum
1/3 cup packed brown sugar
1 tbsp butter
½ tsp cinnamon
Pinch nutmeg or mace
8 firm, ripe bananas

In saucepan, combine juice, rum, sugar, butter, cinnamon and nutmeg. Heat gently, stirring until sugar is dissolved. Peel bananas, cut in half lengthwise and place in buttered baking dish large enough to hold bananas in a single layer. Spoon rum sauce over bananas. Bake in 350 F oven for 8 to 10 minutes or until heated through. Serves 8

CHOCOLATE TIPPED TEA TARTS

1/3 cup margarine
4 oz softened cream cheese
1 cup flour
2 tbsp sugar
¼ cup raspberry jam
3 squares semi-sweet chocolate

Cream margarine and cheese in bowl. Add flour and sugar, mix well. Form dough in a ball then roll into a rectangle on lightly floured surface - not too thick or too thin. Cut into 2½-inch squares. Spoon ½ teaspoon raspberry jam on centers. Moisten edges of each pastry with water. Fold dough over filling to form triangles. Fork crimp edges to seal. Place on ungreased cookie sheet and bake at 425°F for 8 minutes. Cool, then dip one corner into melted chocolate. Makes 24

CARAMEL CHOCOLATE CAKE

14 oz caramels (75 to 80)
1 can sweetened condensed milk
½ cup butter
2/3 cup vegetable oil
4 squares chopped unsweetened chocolate
1½ cups water
2 cups sugar
2 eggs
2½ cups flour
1 tsp salt
1 tsp baking soda
2 tsp vanilla
1½ cups chopped toasted walnuts

In saucepan combine caramels, milk and butter. On medium heat, stir until melted and smooth. Set aside. Melt oil and chocolate in large saucepan. Add water, sugar, eggs, flour, salt, baking soda and vanilla to chocolate mixture. Beat 2 minutes with fork until creamy. Spread half batter in greased 13 x 9 inch cake pan. Bake 350°F, 15 minutes. Remove from oven and spoon caramel mixture evenly over cake. Spread remaining batter evenly over caramel. Sprinkle with nuts. Return to oven and bake 40 minutes or until cake springs back when touched in the center. Cool before cutting.

THE CONCEPTION TOURIST INN

General Delivery
Conception Harbour
NF A0A 1Z0
(709) 229-3988
No. 5 on map, page 6

Follow the Conception Bay Highway, Route 60, and it will lead you to the door step of The Conception Tourist Inn. Don't go any further because when you walk into their sitting room you get that at home country feeling. Is it because of the family coat of arms above the fireplace, the polished wooden furniture, the luxurious guest rooms or the smell of bread baking in the kitchen? Early morning, wake up to the aroma of coffee brewing and enjoy a hearty breakfast. Traditional meals to exotic cuisine available on request, but let them know in advance.

During your stay locate the beached whaler, then, visit the museum and historic railway station. Your coastal driveway is dotted by picturesque fishing villages such as Bacon Cove - a haven for naturalists, artists, and divers. Try your hand at cod jigging or go out whale watching. Ask to hear the story about Father Duffy's Well? At the end of the day, kick up your heels at the local night spots located nearby.

Luxury lodging in a bed and breakfast atmosphere!

HEAVENLY CHOCOLATE CHEESECAKE

2 cups vanilla wafers, finely crushed
1 cup ground toasted almonds
½ cup butter
½ cup sugar

CRUST: In large bowl, combine vanilla wafer crumbs, almonds, butter, sugar and mix well. Pat firmly into 9-inch spring form pan, covering bottom and 2 inches up the sides. Set aside.

2 cups milk chocolate morsels or chips
½ cup milk
1 envelope unflavoured gelatine
2 8-oz packages cream cheese, softened
½ cup sour cream
½ tsp almond extract
½ cup heavy cream whipped

CHEESECAKE: Melt chocolate over hot (not boiling) water. Stir until smooth. Set aside. Pour milk into small sauce pan. Sprinkle gelatin on top. Set aside for 1 minute. Cook over low heat, stirring constantly until gelatin dissolves. Set aside. In large bowl combine cream cheese, sour cream and melted chocolate; beat until fluffy. Beat in gelatin mixture and almond extract. Fold in whipped cream. Pour into prepared pan. Chill until firm (about 3 hours). Run knife around edge of cake to separate from pan and remove sides. Garnish.

This is one of Marg's great recipes. Chocoholics, add this one to your list of favourites!

CHOCOLATE CARROT CAKE

4 eggs
1½ sugar
1 cup oil
½ cup orange juice
1 tsp vanilla
2 cups flour
2 tsp baking soda
1 tsp salt
¼ cup cocoa
1 tsp cinnamon
2 cups grated carrots
1 cup coconut

Beat eggs. Add sugar, then oil, juice and vanilla. Stir in dry ingredients, carrots and coconut. Spoon into greased or floured bundt or tube pan. Bake at 350°F for 55 to 60 minutes.

QUICK METHOD: Combine eggs, oil, juice and whole carrots in blender. Stir into dry ingredients. Spoon into greased or floured baking pan and bake as above.

LIGHT CREAM CHEESE ICING

1 small package nutri-whip
1 cup icing sugar
4 oz cream cheese, room temperature

Beat nutri-whip. Add sugar gradually, then add softened cream cheese. Spread icing on top and down sides of cake.

BLUEBERRY COFFEE CAKE

2 tbsp margarine
½ cup brown sugar
1½ tsp cinnamon
1 tbsp flour

TOPPING: Combine ingredients and set aside.

¾ cup margarine
¾ cup sugar
1 egg
1 cup sour cream
1 tsp vanilla
2 cups flour
1 tsp baking powder
1 tsp baking soda
¼ tsp salt
2 cups fresh blueberries

BATTER: In a large bowl, cream margarine and sugar until light and fluffy. Add egg and blend well. Stir in sour cream and vanilla. Combine flour, baking powder, baking soda and salt. Add to batter. Blend well. Spread ⅔ of batter into lightly greased 9-inch spring form pan. Top with berries. Drop spoonfuls of remaining batter over berries, spread until smooth. Sprinkle with topping mixture. Bake at 350°F for 60 to 70 minutes. Serves 12 *Substitute raspberries, strawberries or apples for blueberries.*

ACKERMAN'S BED AND BREAKFAST

General Delivery
Glovertown, NF
A0G 2L0
(709) 533-2811/2810
No. 14 on map, page 6

Flags of tradition! For years Caleb and Dorothy have been welcoming guests from all over the world to Ackerman's Hospitality Home, only 5 minutes off the main highway. Outside the patriotic colors are blowing in the wind... Inside the aroma of freshly baked cookies make you hungry... You feel at home!

Historically, Glovertown, was a prominent location where men like my grandfather built the large wooden schooners that sailed the icy coastal waters of Labrador. Today, shipbuilding continues... with modern technology and steel.

Make it a part of your heritage, and launch your boat in these renown waters. Go out the tickle and boil lobster on the beaches! Search for mussels! Fly fish for salmon off Doctor's Rock on the Terra Nova River. Terra Nova National Park nearby offers picnic areas, hiking, and horseback riding. Ocean ice skate for miles, cross-country ski and skidoo. You will not be able to stop your toe from tapping and foot from stomping to songs like "I'se the B'y" at the annual Newfoundland Day festival.

Great conversation and warm hospitality year round!

DOROTHY'S JAM JAMS

1 cup dates (cup up)
¼ cup brown sugar
Vanilla

FILLING: Boil all ingredients together for 15 minutes. Cool while making the rest of the recipe.

¾ cup butter
1¼ cup brown sugar
2 eggs
1 tsp vanilla
3 cups flour
1 tsp baking soda
1 tsp cream of tartar
Pinch of salt

Cream butter and sugar. Stir in eggs and vanilla. Add dry ingredients. Mix well and roll out. Cut circles or any shape you like with cookie cutter. Put cooled date filling in between. Bake at 350°F for 12 minutes.

Dorothy often makes these cookies using an apple filling. Another delectable delight!

HOLIDAY RIBBON JELLY

1 package red jelly
½ cup boiling water
½ cup cold water

RED: Set jelly with hot water, then stir in cold water. Pour in greased loaf pan. Make custard while jelly is setting.

2 cups milk
3 tsp sugar
1 tsp vanilla
1 package gelatin
¼ cup cold water

WHITE CUSTARD: Heat milk until hot (do not boil). Stir in sugar and vanilla. Dissolve gelatin in cold water. Add to milk and stir well. Allow to cool. Pour over red jelly. Make green jelly next.

1 package lime jelly
¾ boiling water
¾ cup cold water

GREEN: Set jelly in hot water, then stir in cold water. When partially set, pour over white custard. Remove from pan when jelly is set. Serves 6 to 8

HEART'S DELIGHT DESSERT

2 eggs
¾ cup sugar
1 cup flour
1 tsp baking powder
1 tbsp butter
1 tsp vanilla
1 cup hot milk
Dash of salt
1 tbsp apple juice
Partridgeberry jam
Sliced bananas

Beat eggs, add sugar gradually and beat until fluffy. Fold in sifted dry ingredients. Add butter and vanilla to milk and fold into egg mixture. Pour in pan and bake at 300°F for 35 to 45 minutes. Remove from oven. Just before serving sprinkle apple juice over top. Layer with partridgeberry jam and bananas.

COCONUT ORANGE DROPS

1 egg white
1/3 cup icing sugar
½ tsp finely chopped orange rind
1¼ cups shredded coconut

In a medium bowl, beat egg white until frothy using a whisk. Stir in sugar, orange rind and coconut. Drop large teaspoons of mixture on non-stick cookie sheet and flatten to 1 to 1½-inches. Bake in oven about 275°F to 300°F for 18 minutes or until golden.

PEGGY'S HOSPITALITY HOME

P. O. Box 39
Jackson's Arm, NF
A0K 3H0
(709) 459-3333/3136
No. 17 on map, page 6

Ever jig a squid? a codfish? or catch a caplin in your hands? Well, White Bay is a place where fishermen gather, and nestled in Jackson's Arm is Peggy's Hospitality Home. Her charmingly decorated guest home is the best local place to stay... complete with the finest home cooking around, especially her fresh home made bread. Upon request, she will make you any traditional Newfoundland meal your heart desires.

Fun begins when the schools of caplin arrive in June and boats from all around go out to harvest these tiny silvery fish. You can catch caplin rolling on the beach at Godfathers Cove. Have you ever had your picture taken kissing a codfish? Squid-jigging season starts in August but, be careful you don't squirt yourself. Take your catch home or have it prepared for your supper.

In the back woods, there are many hiking, cross-country skiing and snowshoeing trails. Springtime ice floes fill the harbour. Don't forget Come Home Year.

Make memories to last a lifetime!

LIGHT PINEAPPLE SQUARES

1 cup flour
1 tsp baking powder
¼ tsp salt
¼ cup margarine (cholesterol free)
1 egg, separated
¼ cups 2% milk
14-oz can unsweetened crushed pineapple
2 tbsp cornstarch
2 tsp rum extract
1 tsp vanilla
¼ tsp cream of tartar
1 tbsp sugar
1 cup unsweetened shredded coconut

BOTTOM LAYER: Combine flour, baking powder and salt. Cut in butter until mixture is crumbly. Beat egg yolk and milk with fork, stir into crumbs. Press evenly onto bottom of lightly greased 8-inch square cake pan.

MIDDLE LAYER: Combine pineapple and juice, and cornstarch in a saucepan, mix well. Stir over medium heat until mixture boils and thickens. Stir in rum extract and vanilla. Pour over first layer.

TOP LAYER: Beat egg white and tartar until frothy. Add sugar, beat until soft peaks form. Fold in coconut. Spread evenly over pineapple layer. Press down lightly with fork. Bake 30 minutes at 350°F. Makes 30

"A dessert for those who care about their health," says Peggy. A sugar watcher's delight!

PARTRIDGEBERRY BARS

½ cup butter
1 cup flour
1 cup lightly packed brown sugar
1 cup rolled oats
1½ cups partridgeberry jam

Cut butter into flour, sugar and rolled oats to make crumbly texture. Press half into prepared pan. Spread with partridgeberry jam. Cover with remaining crumbs and pat smooth. Bake at 375°F for 35 minutes or until lightly browned. Cool and cut into bars.

ROLLED OATS SHORTBREAD

2½ cups rolled oats
½ cup brown sugar
1 cup butter
1 cup flour

Cream butter, add sugar and rolled oats. Mix until quite sticky. Add flour. Roll out ¼-inch thick. Cut with unique shaped cookie cutters. Bake at 350°F until golden brown.

CHERRY CREAM MARSHMALLOW COOKIES

1 cup coconut
12 cherries, cut in small pieces
1 tin fresh cream
1½ to 2 cups miniature marshmallows (colored)

Mix all ingredients together. Form into balls and roll in coconut. Makes 2 to 3 dozen

CHOCOLATE MICE COOKIES

1 cup peanut butter
1 cup icing sugar
¼ cup butter
1 cup coconut
¼ cup finely chopped walnuts
2 cups rice crispie cereal
½ bar parowax
1 10-oz package semi-sweet chocolate chips

Cook peanut butter, sugar, coconut and nuts over low to moderate heat in saucepan to combine well. Add rice crispies. Shape into logs or round shape. Allow to cool, the cooler the better. Melt semi-sweet chocolate chips and parowax together. Dip cookies into chocolate mixture. Place on wax paper to cool. *Be careful not to burn chocolate.*

COCOA CHERRY SNOWBALLS

6 tsp cocoa and 2 tbsp butter
  (or 4 squares unsweetened chocolate)
1 tin sweetened condensed milk
2 cups graham wafers crumbs
1 cup coconut
10 cherries cut in quarters

Melt butter in double boiler and mix in cocoa. Stir in sweetened milk. Pour mixture over wafer crumbs and mix. Chill mixture. Form 1-inch balls. Put cherry piece in center. Roll in coconut. Makes 3 dozen

MONROE HOUSE

8A Forest Road
St. John's, NF A1C 2B9
(709) 754-0610
No. 3 on map, page 6

Monroe House, located on a quiet tree-lined avenue, was home to The Honourable Walter S. Monroe, former Prime Minister of Newfoundland. Ships laid hardwood floors run throughout the house and grace the living and dining rooms' rich mahogany furniture. Bedroom furnishings are from the Victorian era and all guest rooms, including the one with the old-fashioned iron bed, have private four-piece bathrooms. Charming decor of colourful floral print bedding, wall coverings and draperies are accented with beautiful artwork, exquisite figurines and other personal touches to surround you in an elegant and relaxing atmosphere.

Guests enjoy a gourmet breakfast, served on bone china, and garnished with fresh fruits of the season.

Within walking distance of four major hotels and the convention centre. Nearby tourist attractions include: City Hall, Signal Hill, Memorial Stadium, central business district, shopping, restaurants, art galleries, museums, hiking trails and the waterfront. Cats in residence.

Elegance and warm hospitality!

SUGARED MOLASSES and RAISIN WONDERS

¾ cup shortening
1 cup granulated sugar
¼ cup molasses
1 egg
2 cups all-purpose flour
2 tsp baking soda
1 tsp cinnamon
½ tsp cloves
½ tsp ginger
¼ tsp salt
1 cup black raisins
Granulated sugar

Cream shortening and sugar in a large bowl on medium speed of electric mixer until light and fluffy. Add molasses and egg. Continue to beat while mixing dry ingredients. Combine flour, baking soda, spices and salt. Add to creamed mixture and mix well with beaters. Remove beaters and stir in raisins using a spoon. (Slightly less than a cup is better than slightly more; they tend to fall out of the mixture.) Shape dough into 1-inch balls. Roll in sugar to coat liberally. Place on a greased baking sheet and bake at 350°F for 10 to 12 minutes, or until set.

The cookies flatten and spread during baking, forming an interesting marbled look. Makes about 3 dozen cookies for freezing, perhaps the only way to keep them around. A Munroe House favourite!

RASPBERRY PUNCH

2 cups raspberry juice
¼ cup sugar
1 tsp cornstarch
1 to 2-inch cinnamon stick
1 cup orange juice
¾ cup grape juice

Boil raspberry juice with sugar, cornstarch and spice. When cool, add juices. Serve over cracked ice or freeze and serve as sherbet.

NEWFOUNDLAND TEA PUNCH

2 cups strong tea
1 cup sugar
1 cup orange juice
1 cup cranberry juice
½ cup lemon juice
1 cup pineapple juice
Ginger ale

Heat tea and sugar until sugar is dissolved. Add rest of ingredients, except ginger ale. Cool when ready to serve. Add ginger ale to taste. Pour into punch bowl adding ice or over ice ring made by putting water into a mold and scattering red and green cherries before freezing.

BLUEBERRY TEA

Slice of orange
¾ oz amaretto liqueur
¾ oz grand marnier liqueur
Hot strong tea

Drop orange in bottom of brandy snifter glass, pour in liqueurs. Serve tea in teapot on the side; pour ½ to ¾ cup of tea in glass. *The tea will dilute the sweetness.* Serves 1

SKIPPER'S COFFEE

Lemon slices
2 tsp sugar
1 oz screech
Hot, strong black coffee
Whipping or fresh cream

Rub glass rim with lemon. Put sugar in bowl; dip the rim in it. Pour screech into the glass. Fill with coffee, stir well, float cream on top. Serves 1

BLUEBERRY WINE

2 qts blueberries
4 qts boiling water
6 cups sugar per gallon of juice
3 cups prunes
1 package yeast

Add boiling water to berries and crush them. Bring to a boil and cook 10 minutes. Strain juice and add sugar per gallon of juice. Boil 5 minutes. Cool to lukewarm, add prunes and yeast. Cover with cloth and let stand in a warm place for 2 months. Strain, bottle and cork.

SALT WATER TAFFY

2 cups sugar
1 cup light corn syrup
1½ tsp salt
1 cup water
2 tbsp butter
¼ tsp oil of peppermint
7 drops of green food coloring

Combine sugar, syrup, salt, water in 2-quart saucepan. Cook slowly, steadily stirring to dissolve sugar. Without stirring, bring to hard ball stage (265°F). Remove from heat, stir in remaining ingredients. Pour into buttered 15½ x 10½ x 1-inch pan. Cool until comfortable enough to handle. Butter hands; gather taffy into a ball and pull. When light in color and hard to pull, cut in quarters; pull each into strands about ½-inch thick. With buttered scissors, quickly snip into small pieces. Wrap each piece in wax paper. Makes 1¼ pounds.

PEPPERMINT TURKISH DELIGHT

3 tbsp unflavoured gelatin
1 cup cold water
2 cups sugar
½ cup hot water
green food coloring
A few drops peppermint extract

Soften gelatin in ½ cup cold water. Boil sugar in hot water. Add gelatin, simmer 20 minutes. Add extract, coloring and remaining cold water. Pour in loaf pan about ½ to 1-inch deep. When cold, cut into squares and roll in icing sugar.

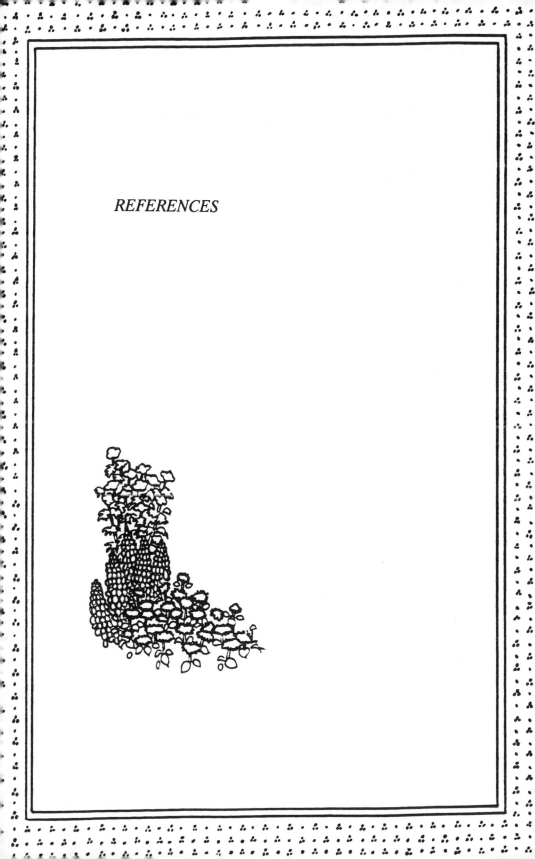

REFERENCES

BED and BREAKFAST, HOSPITALITY HOMES, and COUNTRY INNS

ACKERMAN'S BED and BREAKFAST   (709)   533-2810
General Delivery   533-2811
Glovertown, NF A0G 2L0

Hosts:	Caleb and Dorothy Ackerman
Open:	Year round
Map:	No. 14, page 6
Writeup:	Page 86
Recipe:	Page 87

A GOWER STREET HOUSE   (709)   754-0047
180 Gower Street
St. John's, NF A1C 1P9

Hosts:	Leonard, Kimberly, David
Open:	Year round
Map:	No. 2, page 6
Writeup:	Page 16
Recipe:	Page 17

BEACHY COVE BED and BREAKFAST   (709)   895-2920
P. O. Box 159
Portugal Cove, NF A0A 3K0

Hosts:	Doug and Brenda Cole
Open:	Year round
Map:	No. 4, page 6
Writeup:	Page 20
Recipe:	Page 21

BONNE ESPÉRANCE HOUSE   (709)   726-3835
20 Gower Street
St. John's, NF A1C 1N1

Hostess:	Ann Bell
Open:	Year round
Map:	No. 1, page 6
Writeup:	Page 12
Recipe:	Page 13

CARMANVILLE OLDE INN   (709)   534-2544
P. O. Box 16   534-2825
Carmanville, NF A0G 1N0

Hostess:	Joan Hicks
Open:	Year round
Map:	No. 15, page 6
Writeup:	Page 38
Recipe:	Page 39

CLUETT'S HOSPITALITY HOME   (709)   826-2665
17 Church Street
Garnish, NF A0E 1T0

Hostess:	Bertha Cluett
Open:	Year round
Map:	No. 8, page 6
Writeup:	Page 66
Recipe:	Page 67

EDGEWATER INN BED and BREAKFAST   (709)   634-7026
14 Forest Drive   634-3474
Steady Brook, NF A2H 2N2

Hosts:	Mildred and Trevor Bennett
Open:	Year round
Map:	No. 19, page 6
Writeup:	Page 28
Recipe:	Page 29

KENEALLY MANOR BED and BREAKFAST (709)   596-1221
8 Patrick Street
Carbonear, NF A0A 1T0

Hostess:	Janice Green
Open:	Year round
Map:	No. 6, page 6
Writeup:	Page 32
Recipe:	Page 33

MARY'S BED and BREAKFAST   (709)   681-2210
Little Port Road, Lark Harbour   (off season)   789-3642
(Mail: P. O. Box 231,
Corner Brook, NF A2H 6C9)

Hosts:	Mary and Eric Humber
Open:	Seasonally
Map:	No. 20, page 6
Writeup:	Page 74
Recipe:	Page 75

MONROE HOUSE   (709)   754-0610
8A Forest Road
St. John's, NF A1C 2B9

Hosts:	Jeff and Dawn Levitz
Open:	Year round
Map:	No. 3, page 6
Writeup:	Page 94
Recipe:	Page 95

PARKSIDE INN   (709)   464-2151
P. O. Box 132
Port Rexton, NF A0C 2H0

Hostess:	Christine Whelan
Open:	Year round
Map:	No. 11, page 6
Writeup:	Page 42
Recipe:	Page 43

PEACE COVE INN   (709)   464-3738
Trinity East, NF   464-3419
(Mail: P. O. Box 48,   (off season)   781-2255
Paradise, NF A1L 1C4)

Hosts:	Art and Louise Andrews
Open:	Seasonally
Map:	No. 10, page 6
Writeup:	Page 48
Recipe:	Page 49

PEGGY'S HOSPITALITY HOME   (709)   459-3333
P. O. Box 39   459-3136
Jackson's Arm, NF A0K 3H0

Hostess:	Peggy Jones
Open:	Year round
Map:	No. 17, page 6
Writeup:	Page 90
Recipe:	Page 91

PINSENT'S BED and BREAKFAST   (709)   677-3021
17 Church Street
Eastport, NF A0G 1Z0

Hosts:	Walter and Lillian Pinsent
Open:	Year round
Map:	No. 13, page 6
Writeup:	Page 78
Recipe:	Page 79

RIVERSIDE LODGE (TOURIST HOME)   (709)   464-3780
Site 3, Box 9   464-3578
Trouty, NF A0C 2S0

Hosts:	Annette and Lloyd Miller
Open:	Seasonally
Map:	No. 12, page 6
Writeup:	Page 70
Recipe:	Page 71

SEASIDE LODGE BED and BREAKFAST   (709)   535-6305
341 Main Street
Lewisporte, NF A0G 3A0

Hosts:	Naomi Kinden and Vincent Murray
Open:	Year round
Map:	No. 16, page 6
Writeup:	Page 60
Recipe:	Page 61

THE CONCEPTION TOURIST INN   (709)   229-3988
General Delivery
Conception Harbour, NF A0A 1Z0

Hosts:	Marg and Paul O'Driscoll
Open:	Year round
Map:	No. 5, page 6
Writeup:	Page 82
Recipe:	Page 83

THE "OLDE HOUSE" BED and BREAKFAST (709)   454-0005
9 American Drive   (off season)   454-3794
St. Anthony, NF A0K 4S0

Hostess:	Pauline Parrill
Open:	Seasonally
Map:	No. 18, page 6
Writeup:	Page 56
Recipe:	Page 57

THE STATION HOUSE   (709)   466-2036
P. O. Box 117   466-2008
Clarenville, NF A0E 1J0

Hostess:	Una Durant
Open:	Year round
Map:	No. 9, page 6
Writeup:	Page 24
Recipe:	Page 25

WHALEN'S HOSPITALITY HOME   (709)   338-2506
P. O. Box 46
Branch, NF A0B 1E0

Hosts:	Rosemary and Art Whalen
Open:	Year round
Map:	No. 7, page 6
Writeup:	Page 52
Recipe:	Page 53

MY TRAVEL NOTES

RECIPE INDEX

METRIC CONVERSION TABLES

Abbreviations

tsp .... teaspoon   qt ... quart
tbsp .. tablespoon   g ..... gram
oz ...... ounce   ml .. millitre
lb ...... pound   l ...... litre
pt ...... pint

Spoons

¼ tsp ..... 1 ml
½ tsp ..... 2 ml
1 tsp ...... 5 ml
1 tbsp .. 15 ml
2 tbsp .. 25 ml
3 tbsp .. 50 ml

Cups

¼ cup ...... 50 ml
⅓ cup ...... 75 ml
½ cup .... 125 ml
⅔ cup ... 150 ml
¾ cup .... 175 ml
1 cup ..... 250 ml

Weight

1 oz .... 30 g
2 oz .... 55 g
3 oz .... 85 g
4 oz .... 125 g
8 oz .... 250 g
12 oz .. 375 g
16 oz .. 500 g

Liquid Measure

1 tsp .... 20 drops
1 tbsp .. 3 tsp
1 oz ..... 2 tbsp
1 cup ... 8 oz
1 cup ... 16 tbsp
2 cups .. 1 pint

Baking Pans and Casseroles Dishes

8 x 8-inch, 20 x 20 cm, 2l (square)
9 x 9-inch, 22 x 22 cm, 2.5l (square)
9 x 13-inch, 22 x 33 cm, 4l (rectangular)
10 x 15-inch, 25 x 38 cm, 1.2l (rectangular)
14 x 17-inch, 35 x 43 cm, 1.5l (rectangular)
8 x 2-inch, 20 x 5 cm, 2l (round)
9 x 2-inch, 22 x 5 cm, 2.5l (round)
8 x 4 x 3-inch, 20 x 10 x 7 cm, 1.5l (loaf)
9 x 5 x 3-inch, 23 x 12 x 7cm, 2l (loaf)
10 x 4½-inch, 25 x 11 cm, 5l (tube)

Oven Temperatures: Faharenheit (°F) and Celcius (°C)

°F	°C	°F	°C
200	100	350	180
225	110	375	190
250	120	400	200
275	140	425	220
300	150	450	230
325	160	475	240

MY RECIPE NOTES

MY FAVOURITE RECIPES

Recipe Name	Page

GIFT GIVING MADE EASY!

The perfect souvenir or gift - Birthdays, Mother's Day, Christmas or any occasion!

Blueberry Press will send this book with a complimentary gift card and your personal message to your friend, relative or any person you choose. If you prefer, provide us with your handwritten message on your gift card, and we will enclose it with your gift.

To order copies, please use Order Form on reverse side of this page.

ORDER FORM

NEWFOUNDLAND: A Taste of Home by Rosalind Crocker $12.00 each
       Includes GST
       Shipping charge is $2.50 per copy (Canada only)
       Within Newfoundland add $1.44 PST per copy

$12.00 + ($1.44 PST, + $2.50 = $____ x ___ copies = if applicable) (shipping)		$

I would like to receive ___ copies of this book. Enclosed is my cheque/money order for $_____ made payable to BLUEBERRY PRESS.

Name _____
Street _____
City _____
Province _____ Postal Code _____

Prices subject to change without notice. Delivery 2 to 4 weeks.

Send Order Form and Payment to: **Blueberry Press**
                                    P. O. Box 612-A
                                    Mount Pearl, NF Canada A1N 2X1

. . . .
SEND TO MY FRIEND: (Please print clearly)

Name _____
Street _____
City _____
Province _____ Postal Code _____

____ My personalized gift card is enclosed, please send with gift to my friend.

____ Blueberry Press, please send your complimentary gift card stating this message:
      _____
      _____

. . . .
SEND TO MY FRIEND: (Please print clearly)

Name _____
Street _____
City _____
Province _____ Postal Code _____

____ My personalized gift card is enclosed, please send with gift to my friend.

____ Blueberry Press, please send your complimentary gift card stating this message:
      _____
      _____